Miracle at Large

Ricky Sinclair
with Gerald Johnston

Printed by Baker Printing

Baker, Louisiana

Library of Congress Catalog Number 97-065926
ISBN 1-928772-08-0
Ninth Printing

Printed in the United States
By Baker Printing Co., Inc.

This book is dedicated to the ones who have been instrumental in changing Ricky's life.

First, to God by whom all things are made possible.

Second, to Jeannie who has stuck by Ricky through thick and thin.

And finally, to every person in the field of law enforcement and criminal corrections- those who helped Ricky lose his old life and find his new one.

Jesus said, *"For whoever desires to save his life will lose it, and whoever loses his life for My sake will find it."*
(Matthew 16:25 NKJ)

Contents

Foreword

I want to take a few minutes to introduce the main character of this story. His name is Ricky Sinclair. I knew Ricky about 20 years ago when we attended school together in Woodville, Mississippi. Although I had heard some things about him over the years, I hadn't seen Ricky since those early school days. A mutual friend of ours told me that Ricky had been saved. In February 1996, 1 decided to stop by his house in Wakefield, Louisiana, for a visit. He answered the door saying, "Hey! How are you doing? How about Jesus?"

Needless to say, Ricky Sinclair is a Christian well, needless to anyone who has seen Ricky in the last 10 years. Prior to his experience with Jesus 10 years ago, Ricky Sinclair was everything but a Christian. This book takes you on a journey through his life: drugs, jail, escape from jail, return to jail, his life changing salvation experience, prison, and some post conversion life experiences.

Ricky has been a great friend to me. He is truly one of those friends that I can count on one hand. I am certain that God has put us back together for a reason, and I know that this book is a large part of that reason. I was unemployed in February when I stopped by to see Ricky. He was a great encouragement to me. I went to church with him the next day, and he urged me to become a part of their congregation. Ricky also teaches Bible study in his home, and I soon became a regular part of their group. Within a couple of months, he had secured me a job with his employer in Baton Rouge, Louisiana. In June he helped me pack up and move to Baton Rouge.

Between work and church, I've really spent a lot of time with Ricky. I've really gotten to know him well. I've learned that he's solid for Jesus. Always! Everywhere! He's not flaky, shaky, or faky. He's real, and he never fails to mention Jesus to anyone. If you've talked to Ricky over the last 10 years, I'm sure that he's asked you about Jesus. He'll say something like: " Do you know jesus?" If your answer is no, he'll proceed to tell you how Jesus has changed his life. If your answer is yes, he'll say: "Do you know how to lead someone in a sinner's prayer?" He's truly a general in the Army of God.

A few months ago, Ricky and I went deep sea fishing out of Fourchon on the Louisiana coast. I tell you this, Ricky is a bona fide tough guy. He'll fish for 48 hours straight. No sleep! He has his own boat and fishes 30 miles out. It's a regular routine for him, but I haven't been back.

Along with being bold and tough, he also has a heart full of love. We picked up a hitch hiker one day while working together. Ricky gave the guy a $20 bill and then shared his personal testimony. I also shared my testimony. Ricky led him in a sinner's prayer, gave him a Bible, and then drove him to his destination, Natchez, Mississippi- a mere 120 miles out of our way. No problem. This is just normal, everyday stuff for Ricky. On another day, we met a lady that had fallen on hard times. She didn't have any food for her kids. We drove her to the grocery store, let her shop for 30 minutes, and then Ricky paid for her groceries.

Ricky is really blessed. He has a great wife and two wonderful kids. He has a good job, works hard, and uses his money to bless others. During the summer, I saw him give a car to someone. He's unbelievably generous but likewise blessed. He recently took legal custody of a teenager who was in need of a dad. In order to get custody, Jeannie (Ricky's wife) had to go see the same judge that had sentenced Ricky to prison years ago. I'm sure that it was quite a meeting.

Being familiar with Ricky's testimony, I began to encourage him to write a book. He wasn't too keen on the idea at first; he didn't think that anybody would be interested. I argued that his story was very interesting and told him I would write it. He finally agreed. We bought a tape recorder and started writing. Our objective from the onset has been to glorify God. We also wanted the book to be clear, concise, and accurate. I believe that we have achieved that goal.

Though others have been through similar experiences, it is the ending that makes this a great story. We surely hope that you enjoy reading it, and that you find it to be in keeping with the mission that Jesus gave to the church:

"....to open their eyes and to turn them from darkness to light, and from the power of Satan to God, that they may receive forgiveness of sins and an inheritance among those who are sanctified by faith in Me."

(Acts 26:18 NKJ)

Ricky and his family, 2002

"Busted"

"Man, look at all the cops! They're everywhere! We've got to get out of here! Man, go! Go! Go! Go!"

"Where to, Ricky?"

"I don't know! Man... I'm busted! Did you see all those cops?"

Well, that was the situation when I arrived at my house in West Feliciana Parish one afternoon in 1986. Swat teams, state police, surveillance teams, and local police had kicked my door down, and they weren't playing. I had sold some pot to a friend of mine that morning, but had no idea that he was in trouble with the law. He was looking at some time, and had consequently made a deal. The deal was that he was turning state's evidence and the evidence was my dope. I had been smuggling drugs out of Mexico for many years and the West Feliciana police wanted me badly. When I arrived at my house and saw all the commotion, I hit the road running.

I went to a friend's house to regroup, to develop a plan and, of course, to get high. The plan was to sneak back home at midnight to get Jeannie, my wife, and Stirling, my one year old son. Yeah, this will be cool. We'll move and I'll use my alias, James Louis Winnfield. I traded my Chevy truck for a green T-Bird and then sent word to Jeannie that I would be coming to get her. I felt confident that this would work.

That night I carried out the plan. It did work. Jeannie was packed and ready. We were off and running. We went to Baton Rouge and rented a motel room. I made a few phone calls and hooked up with a couple of my buddies down there. I needed their help; we needed somewhere to stay for a while.

Later, four or five of my friends showed up at our motel room. We partied: drank, got high, got the munchies. We were really hungry, but there wasn't anything to eat. So, my buddies and I decided to run up to the local Taco Bell.

We left Jeannie and Stirling at the motel. We piled into my green T-Bird and lit out for the grub. John drove. We parked at the 7-11 store next door to the Taco Bell. We were almost through burning a doobie when a guy, a friend of one of my buddies, walked up and leaned in the window. The next second we were surrounded by undercover narcotics agents. It happened so fast. My heart was racing. I had to think up something quick.

"All right, everybody out of the car. Turn around, put your hands against the car, legs spread."

"What's your name boy?" one of the cops aske me.

"James Louis Winnfield, Sir."

"Where do you live?"

"At 921 Lanier Street, Apartment 951."

"Let me see your driver's license. What do you do for a living?"

"Sir, I do independent mechanic work, and I just lost my driver's license three days ago. I haven't even had a chance to get another one yet. Life's been hectic lately, Sir. I don't even know why I'm hanging out with people like this. I came from a real good family, Sir."

It turned out that Mike and John were as hot as I was; the cops had been looking for them. As the police were escorting them off, I yelled out to John and asked if he wanted me to drive "his car" home. He said yes. The officers had no objections. It was incredible-things had gone so smoothly. There I was, a natural born con artist, driving off in what they thought was someone else's car, and without a driver's license. Man, I could lie with the best of 'em.

I drove back to the motel and told Jeannie what had happened. She could hardly believe it. We discussed our situation; with John and Mike in jail, we were going to need a new plan. But what? Randy! I'll hook up with Randy. Surely he'll put us up till I can sort things out.

We spent that night in our hotel room, and then packed up and headed to Randy's house the next morning. He was glad to see us, but I don't think his wife was too enthused. She didn't care much for our kind of adventure, and to top it off, we were broke. Having no money, I had to risk going back to West Feliciana to harvest my weed. I talked Randy into going with me. That night we headed out for the woods near my house. Randy drove around while I went into the woods with a flashlight and harvested two duffel bags of marijuana. We met up at the appointed time and headed back to his house. Success!

We stayed with Randy for a couple of days, and then it was time to move on. We headed towards New Orleans, selling weed, staying wherever we could. We hung out for a little while with Bobby, a friend of my cousin's on the west bank in New Orleans. While there, I bought an alias, Kent Douglas Smith. I got everything name, social security number, birth certificate-for $75.00.

Things started slowing down in New Orleans, so we left Bobby and headed for Baton Rouge. It was night and the lights on the T-Bird began flittering. We pulled off the interstate on an exit ramp in a town where Marty, another friend, lived. We went by his house and he helped me repair the electrical problem. I explained our situation to him. He suggested that we move to Chalmette. His uncle was getting him a job at a plant down there and he was hopeful that he could get me a job too.

So we went to Chalmette, Louisiana in St. Bernard Parish near New Orleans. Marty rented the cheapest place he could find, a dumpy motel room, but we were grateful to have it. We were broke; our weed had run out. Our son was wearing a bath towel for a diaper and was living off a pint of watered down milk per day. We were skimping by on one turkey ham sandwich per day, but at least we were together and free, no cops.

We met a couple down there and they soon became our friends. Glen introduced us to his girlfriend's ex-husband, Ricky, and his wife, Susie. Ricky and Susie really liked us. They were our kind. Susie made me a fake ID for Kent Douglas Smith, and I used it to get a check cashing card. Glen got me a job as a painter in Violet. Things were going pretty good.

I decided that it was time to move from our dumpy motel room; we had been there long enough. Glen found a small shotgun house for rent. It was a mansion compared to the motel room. I called my mother and asked her to buy my trailer in West Feliciana Parish; she did. She brought $1,500 to us in Chalmette and we put up a deposit on the house, along with the first month's rent, and moved in. Glen moved in with us. He had some living room furniture and a bed. Jeannie dragged home an old single size box spring that she found beside a garbage dumpster. It had a spring poking through the surface on Jeannie's side of course! Ah, home sweet home! We celebrated our new home; Glen and I used the remainder of the money shooting dope.

I soon met some new "business" people. It was time to get things going. We set up shop. I made a few more phone calls and was soon back in business. My new connections sent in 4 Mexicans with a shipment. They stayed at my house with my wife and kid while Glen and I moved the weed. These guys were nobody to play around with. One of Glen's friends had spent some of their money free basing cocaine; he didn't see his kid again, until he paid. Yeah, everything was back to normal: dealing, using, and smuggling. I was a junky who dealt drugs to do drugs, but it was catching up with me fast.

After a few weeks, Glen's girlfriend started freaking me out. She was the type that would rat on you. We moved in with Ricky and Susie for a couple of weeks to get away from her. Finally, I got my connection to front me some money for a deposit on a little house near the airport. We moved again. I liked Glen, but felt safer without him.

One morning in January 1987, 1 went to the bus station and picked up Lialo, a Mexican smuggler who was delivering me 30 pounds of marijuana. Lialo, would stay with me long enough for me to sell enough dope to pay for the shipment, and then he would return to Mexico to get another shipment. He was a sitter, a guerrilla who was there not only to deliver, but also to make sure that I paid. I was a junky, and my habit was expensive. Many times I would be broke when the shipment arrived, and the sitter would hang around for a day or two while I sold enough dope to pay him. That happened to be the situation this day.

At 10:00 p.m. the police rammed through my door with a 4-man ramming bar -what a shocking entrance! One minute we were relaxed watching TV, the next minute there were a dozen cops in my living room. There was no time to react. They were yelling, "On the floor! Everybody! Hands behind your heads! If your hands leave your head, your head leaves your shoulders!"

Busted again. There were seven of us there, plus my one year old son. The police took my child, handcuffed the rest of us, and hauled us to the St. Bernard Parish jail. They later released everyone except Lialo and me, Kent Douglas Smith. We were booked with possession with intent to distribute 14 pounds of marijuana and 1 ounce of ecstasy. Thank goodness for the fake ID and birth certificate. My cousin will bond me out and we'll move again. Well, that's what I thought.

"Well now, Mr. Sinclair," the sergeant said as he walked up to my cell. "Mr. Ricky Sinclair."

My heart dropped. I was speechless. They've really got me; they know who I am. Did he say Ricky Sinclair? He did. They've got me. My heart sank further as I remembered the warrant in West Feliciana Parish. I'm in big trouble. This could mean prison. This will mean prison! What can I do? What will I do? The thoughts were coming fast. I was ghastly afraid. My freedom. God help me. What will I do? These are major charges and now they'll know about West Feliciana Parish. How did they get my name? This is a nightmare.

The Escape

Fear mounted while I was a prisoner in the St. Bernard Parish Jail One of the seven people that was arrested with me had gotten scared during police questioning and had given the police my real name. Now they knew everything.

I had spent 8 months in the parish prison in 1982 for distribution of marijuana, diazepam, and cocaine. I was a repeat offender, an habitual criminal, and it was sure to go heavy against me. The police and my fellow inmates were plaguing me with rumors of life in prison. Even if I only got a few years from the charges in Chalmette, I would still have to face charges in West Feliciana Parish. The magistrate court had set my bond at $22,500 in St. Bernard, and I was ready to make bail. I was tired of being locked up. I was tired of jail food. I missed my family, my freedom, my drugs. I pleaded with my mother, but she wouldn't bail me out.

Thoughts of escape were constantly on my mind. That was my only solution: I had to escape. I found a piece of steel in my cell and used it to saw on the bars. It was going to be a long process to cut through those bars without a saw, but I seemed to have plenty of time. My efforts were futile. I had to make bail!

A portion of my family's estate in West Feliciana Parish had been left to me. I had always been an excellent con artist, so I called my mother and threatened to sell my portion of the estate if she didn't bail me out. It worked; I was finally able to con my mother into paying my bail. So in the middle of April 1987, after eating breakfast and making bail in St. Bernard Parish, two sheriff's deputies from West Feliciana Parish arrived to pick me up. I was released into their custody around noon. They handcuffed me, shackled my legs with leg irons, and drove me back to West Feliciana Parish.

During the ride back, all I could think about was getting out. I was sick and tired of Jail. All I would have to do would be to call my grandmother and get her to pay bail for me in West Feliciana. I was sure that she would; she had always helped me. I'll go to magistrate court, and they'll set the bond. Then, I'll call Grandmother and she'll bail me out. I should be home before dark.

We arrived at St. Francisville in West Feliciana Parish around 2:00 p.m. The first stop was magistrate court. To my dismay the magistrate set my bond at one million dollars, cash no property bonds. They didn't have any plans of letting me go anywhere.

I arrived at the West Feliciana Parish jail around 3:00 p.m. The deputies removed the leg irons and handcuffs. They took finger prints and mug shots. I called Grandmother, but there was nothing she could do. I was at the end of my rope, doomed to a life in prison. I made up my mind: I had to escape.

"Officer, can I use the restroom? I want to wash this ink off my hands."

"Yeah, but make it quick."

I was wearing a black Harley Davidson tee shirt, blue jeans, and a pair of flip flops, nothing else. I went into the restroom and quickly removed the flip flops. Holding them in one hand, I immediately flung the door open with the other. I flew towards the front door with my heart racing ninety to nothing.

Officer James shouted, "Hey, hey, hey! Where you going?"

I dashed past the deputy who was standing at the front door and darted across the parking lot. The deputies were right on my tail. (I believe the only reason Officer James didn't catch me right there in that parking lot was because he was wearing cowboy boots. He's really fast.) There was a chain link fence across the back of the jail yard. I knew the place well; I had resided there before. I hit the fence while running wide open and in one stride was on the other side. The adrenaline was really pumping. I'd never had an experience like this. My heart was pounding. I was a fugitive.

I ran into the woods, still barefooted. Stickers had covered the bottoms of my feet and had gotten between all of my toes. My feet were bleeding in pain, but I continued to run, the adrenaline was still pumping. I ran for about an hour and really covered a lot of ground, but my body was worn out. I would stop and rest for about 15 seconds at the top of each hill and then continue to run.

I nearly stepped on a rattlesnake as I rushed up a large hillside through blackjack vines and briars. The brush was really thick. And then I heard them. The bloodhounds. The Angola Penitentiary search team was on my trail. I was terribly frightened. Unless the dogs lost my trail, I would be caught. I was out in the woods with nowhere to go. I began to run in figure eight patterns to throw the dogs off my trail. My arms, face, and feet were bleeding from running through the briars. The skin was literally being raked off my arms, neck, and face. The dogs continued to bark; they were still a good ways behind me. I kept listening as I ran. And then came the helicopters. They were searching for me from the air. I dove into the brush and briars to keep from being seen; they were directly overhead. The chasers were closing in, but fortunately the afternoon was ticking by. It would be dark soon. I had to hang on till dark.

I ran to the edge of a field. There was a police car on the other side, so I turned and ran back into the woods. I continued running deeper and deeper into the woods. Then I came upon a gravel road and spotted a game warden. I was afraid that I was surrounded. I turned and ran again., I finally. came to a road near the Mississippi River. I decided to wait there till dark and I then cross the road and try to swim across the river.

I laid down near the top of a cliff and waited for dark. There was a creek down below me; I was very thirsty. I wanted some water, but knew that I couldn't move; I had to be extremely still. I could still hear the dogs and hclicopters. I was engulfed with tremendous fear and torment.

As I lay there, I heard the sound of fourwheel drives. I could tell that they were fourwheel drives from the sound of the knobbies on the blacktop. Thcy would go about 50 yards or so and then stop to let a stander (an Angola guard) out. Then they would go another 50 yards or so and let another one out. From the top of the cliff where I was positioned under some briars, I could look across a field and see approximately 15 Angola guards spaced across the field. At that point I was certain that I was surrounded. I knew that the only chance

I had was to lay dormant until they gave up the search. This would surely take days.

I decided that I had better improve my position, so I began to move the leaves from around me. I wanted to have an area that I could lay in without making any noise from moving in the leaves. To keep from being heard, I cleared out the area by moving one leaf at a time. It took a while to get down to the dirt, but I managed to make a clearing. There was nothing left to do but wait.

My figure eight patterns must have worked; the dogs had lost my trail. Fire ants began eating the blood off my body. They were continually on my face, neck, arms, and feet. They were between my toes. I couldn't even swat at them; the guards were so close. At times the guards were within 10 feet. The mosquitoes nearly carried me out of that swamp. I lay in that one spot without water, food or anything for four nights and three days. I was in complete misery!

Nights are pretty cool in Louisiana in April, but I wasn't that cold. My body was literally numb. I began to hallucinate from dehydration. Many strange thoughts came to mind. Maybe they're putting glycerin or something in the air to make me hallucinate. I was plenty scared. I felt like death. At night it felt like there were demons poking at me. I was hallucinating that badly from the lack of water.

Around day two or three, I can't remember exactly which, an Angola guard sat down on the cliff top about 20 feet above where I was lying. I watched him as he opened up a Sprite and drank it. My mind was busy trying to figure out how I could get that Sprite out of his hand. The agony grew!

That guard was so close that I'm still amazed that he didn't see me. There were many times when they almost caught me. Later that same night, I accidentally made some noise and several guards came over to the top of the cliff. They peered down on my position with night sight goggles. They were so close (within 4 feet) that I could even hear them breathing. They must have been wearing some type of mask. The next day I made some noise again and two guards walked over to the cliff top. I had grown up in the woods, so I made some noise like a small animal in the leaves, and the guards just shrugged their shoulders and walked off.

Yes, there were many such instances when they almost had me. Bloodhounds walked all around me, but they never picked up my scent. I leaned up one day and saw a guard with a shotgun standing about 30 feet in front of me. I just eased back down. He never saw me. Several hours later I leaned up again and could see lines of guards in the field. I was right under their noses. I sat them out; I waited them out for four nights and three days. I was fighting for my life and refused to give up. I was a child of the devil, and I was reaping his rewards.

That fourth day I was at the point that it didn't matter whether they shot me or not, I had to get something to drink. I knew that if they were still there when I stood up that fourth day that they would probably blow me away. BUT GOD, as the Bible says, must have intervened and put it on their hearts and minds to back out. When I stood up I didn't see any guards; they had pulled out. I eased down the side of that cliff towards the stagnant creek below. I was so weak that I could hardly walk. The adrenaline that had run through my body during those days had literally worn my body out. My muscles were beyond pain. I drank water from a stagnant hole that was full of mosquito larvae. I could feel those larvae in my throat as I drank, but that water was delicious, the best. I needed it so badly.

It appeared that all of the perimeter guards had been pulled out. I was no longer surrounded. I saw one guard late that afternoon near the Creek. He probably would have caught me if he had stayed in the woods a little longer, but he was pulling out before nightfall.

It was hot during the days and cold at night. It was also very dry. I was hoping that it would rain to give me some fresh water, but it didn't. My body was terribly weak.

Ricky just minutes before the escape

56 Days

I wanted to give up. My body ached. I was hungry, dirty, and tired. I was terrified, confused, and terribly alone. Everything within me said quit, but I couldn't. I was a fugitive, and the police were frightfully upset with me. I couldn't quit. I was afraid that if I turned myself in they would shoot me on sight. I had really been a thorn in their side, and they were plenty mad. They had to be; I couldn't quit.

It had been four and a half days since breakfast at the St. Bernard Parish jail and I was starving. I eased down the creek towards a field that was full of thistles. I used my flip flop to chop down a thistle, then knocked the thorny branches off the hull. I cracked the hull and scraped the meat out with my teeth. It wasn't that bad. I ate another one.

It was late evening, almost dark, so I eased back into the woods and lay down. I was still hallucinating from dehydration. I watched what appeared to be Angola guards putting a net in the trees to catch me. I knew that it was just an hallucination, because they wouldn't need a net to catch me. I was awfully weak. They could easily arrest me with guns or by force, but the hallucination appeared very real. I soon fell asleep.

The next morning I began walking cautiously through the woods in search of anything that might possibly help me. I came up to an old deer stand. It was about 15 feet off the ground, with 4 foot walls and a tin roof. That old deer stand became my home for the next 52 days.

The woods were terribly dry. The only water that I could find was in tiny puddles along the creek bed. Every puddle was hot, dirty, and infested with mosquito larvae, but I was happy to have any water at all. During the first few days, I literally survived off of thistles and that filthy water. My body was too weak for hunting at first. I tried eating some poke salad, but it wasn't edible. The blackberries were just beginning to bloom". I ate them at each stage. I learned that you can eat green and red blackberries without getting sick.

Life was really tough in those woods. I was totally alone. I didn't speak a single word the whole two months I was in those woods. That's a long time to go without speaking. It was one of the most difficult things, the silence. For the most part, the only noises that I heard were from the animals. I went many days without seeing a soul, but I knew that there were still some guards out in those woods with me.

As my body got stronger, I started hunting. Life was primitive. I made a knife out of the top of a cat food can. I used it to skin my prey. I would kill armadillos, cut the backstrap out with my knife, and eat the raw meat right there on the spot. I couldn't build a fire and risk getting caught, so there was no way to cook anything. I ate raw meat from everything that I caught: armadillo, frog, and turtle. The armadillos were the best to eat, but they were the hardest to kill. They're hard to sneak up on, and they're very fast. I would chase them down, and then kill them with a stick. I threw big rocks at deer several times from the deer stand, but never got one. I chased rabbits, but never caught one. I was living like a caveman.

It was wonderful to be out of those fire ants that had put me through so much misery during those first four days. The mosquitoes continued to plague me, but now that the guards weren't close by, I could at least swat at the pesky things. In the deer stand the mosquitoes were not nearly as bad. It wasn't air tight or anything, but the walls did slow them down quite a bit.

Periodically, there were still a few guards around. I was always on the alert. Sometimes the guards would try to trick me into thinking that they were civilian workers out building cattle fences in those woods. They would make noises and say things to try to convince me of this. They were trying to draw me to them, but I never approached anything that they had set up for me. I was very cautious.

I made daily scavenger rounds through the woods in search of food. I made trails which enabled me to always find my way back to the deer stand. It was my home, my shelter. I spent at least 15 out of every 24 hours in that shelter. Having no flashlight or matches, I went to sleep at the first of nightfall and woke up with the animals at daybreak.

I made the best of the situation that I found myself in, and my living conditions gradually improved. The dried up creek bed ran right by my deer stand. There were a few water puddles that weren't completely dried up. I took baths in the largest puddle and drank from the smaller ones.

I had really learned my way around those woods. One day I found a wheat field. The wheat was pretty good food. I weaved some of it into a rope to replace a flip flop strap that had broken. I also made a belt; I had lost a lot of weight and my pants had been slipping down. I was really thin, weighing about 125 pounds, down 35 or so from my usual 160.

During another scavenger round, I found a couple of bulldozer dirt piles where someone had planted some turnip greens. Those turnips really helped and became a regular part of my diet. I later found a fresh garbage dump. It wasn't a large dump, but was one that several families were using. There aren't many luxuries in primitive survival; in fact, this was probably the best one that I found out there - a garbage dump. I browsed through it daily. Needless to say, there was no radio, television, or anything like that out in those woods, but I did find some old books and magazines to read, which probably kept me from going totally crazy.

When I think back on those days, I realize just how good we do have it, and how much we take for granted the good things that we have.

The dump was truly valuable. I found some old boots, a perfect fit, that were very beneficial to me in those woods. I found a blanket, a welcome companion during those cold nights. Among other things, I also found some two liter soft drink bottles that still had flat drink left in them. I picked some blackberries, put them in some empty milk Jugs, and poured the soft drink on the berries. I let them sit for several weeks to allow the sugar from the drinks to cause the berries to ferment. I squeezed the berries while draining the liquid through a screen into another jug. I had successfully made a potent batch of blackberry wine. I say it was potent, but who knows. I was so weak that it wouldn't have taken much to get me drunk.

During the last 30 days of my ordeal, I was drunk every night. I would sit in the deer stand every evening and read magazines while getting drunk. That second month was much more tolerable than the first one. I was waiting them out. I wanted to let plenty of time pass by. My deer stand had turned into a pretty nice place under the circumstances. When it finally did rain, I was high and dry in my shelter. Well, maybe I should say, drunk and dry.

I had several close encounters with rattlesnakes while hunting animals and picking berries. I remember hearing the rattle from one that was right under my feet. Maybe I stepped on him. I'm not sure, but he certainly scared me. If he had bitten me, I would have died for sure.

Another day I saw the biggest rattlesnake that I have ever seen. I tried to kill it for food. I broke a big log over its back, but he never even slowed down. It's a miracle that the rattlesnakes alone didn't take me out. I was really fortunate.

The one good thing that I gained from the whole experience was an understanding of nature. I really became a harmonious part of those woods. It was interesting to live in the wild like that, to observe the animals as a fellow inhabitant for that length of time. The Discovery Channel cannot possibly bring that understanding to you; you have to experience it for yourself. In this high tech society that we live in today, most of us really miss out on experiencing nature firsthand. After being out there like that, I now have a new sense of understanding for the old cliche, "take time to smell the roses." I had a lot of peaceful days out there. I guess a lot of my appreciation for what is good in life came from my experiences during those days. I'm sure that the Garden of Eden was really great. In a way it is a shame that technology is taking us further and further away from it.

Many weeks had passed since I had darted across the parking lot of that jail. As if being without the modern conveniences of home wasn't enough, I was also without any snuff, a habit that I'd had since childhood. I had no television, no stereo, no soap, no shampoo, not even a toothbrush, much less any tooth paste. The clothes that I was wearing could nearly stand up in a corner by themselves. I chipped several teeth while eating thistles. Today, ten years later, my teeth are still stained from those thistles and blackberries.

I spent many hours planning my next move. I didn't want to go back to civilization too soon. I knew that they would be looking for me to return. It would be dangerous to go back, but eventually I would have to. Fearful thoughts came to mind. What if a tornado blew in? I didn't have adequate shelter for that. I had to start thinking about going back. Maybe I could use a storm to my advantage. Yeah, that would be a great time to go back. During a bad storm, no one would be thinking about me. So I waited for a bad storm, but it never came.

One day while walking in the woods, I saw a crew of men from an electric company out working on the power lines. I carefully maneuvered over to a position near them. I sat and watched as they worked. I wanted to sneak over, hide in their truck, and ride in with them. I kept thinking about it. No, that would be too dangerous. I needed a plan, a good plan. I decided to head out towards Highway 61, cross the highway, and make my way back to my mother's house. I had waited long enough. I was malnourished to say the least. I would nearly faint every time I stood up, but was as healthy as possible under the circumstances. It was time to go back to civilization.

A few days later I awoke to a foggy morning: it was time to go back. I headed down my trail that lead to Highway 61. Up ahead I could see some activity. Something moved. I felt sure that it was a stander. I thought that they must have a guard line near the road, so I low crawled through the line. After 50 yards or so, I stood back up and headed towards the road. I took several steps and then ran head on into a guinea wasp nest. They started stinging me in the face. I was scared to slap at them for fear of making noise, so I mashed them into my face. What an ending.

I dashed across the road, unseen. I ran into the woods, then walked up to Rosedown Plantation. I could see the guard house at Rosedown from the edge of those woods. I wanted to go ask the guard if I could use the phone. I waited a minute. My mind ran. What do I look like? Can I even talk? I haven't spoken a single word in nearly two months.

I had to do it. I walked up and asked if I could use the phone. He looked at me real strange. My voice must have sounded really weak. I told him that I had been lost in the woods for several days and really needed to use the phone. He let me. I called my mother and asked her to come get me. She said no. I wasn't surprised. I thanked the guard, and then walked off. I had to find somebody to give me a ride home.

I walked back off into the woods, and started up the creek. I saw some kids up ahead, and one of them took a picture of me. When he took my picture, I ran up to them.

"Hey, I need some help. I got lost a few days ago on the creek. I was out hunting for antique bottles and got lost. Can ya'll help me?"

They led me up to their house, and I went in with them. Their mother was cooking. It smelled great. It was all I could do to keep from asking for some food. Their dad walked up and asked me what I was doing. I explained that I had gotten lost while bottle hunting. I asked him if he would give me a ride home. He couldn't. He was on his way to work, but instructed his wife to take me home. So she and her kids drove me to my mother's house. I still wonder what they would have done if they had known who I really was Ricky Sinclair, a wanted man.

Ricky soon after his capture

Caught

The nightmare was finally over. It would be impossible to ever portray the literal hell that I had just gone through. I had been through a battle. A battle against weather, hunger, dehydration, briars, Angola guards, bloodhounds, helicopters, rattlesnakes, mosquitoes, fire ants, loneliness, and fear. It was finally over. I had won, and it felt great to be home. I thanked the kind lady for the ride.

No one was home, and the house was locked. I went around back and climbed in through an unlocked window. My first stop was the refrigerator. Food! Real food! Leftover barbecued chicken. It was great, simply delicious! I poured a glass of milk. It was the first drink that I had taken from a glass in two months; necessity had become luxury -oh yes, the conveniences of home.

I walked into the bathroom and looked at myself in the mirror for the first time in months. I stared at a morbid man in that mirror. I looked awful. I had a long harsh beard and long ratty hair. My eyes were drawn back deep into my skull. I looked like a skeleton. My face and arms were scarred from running through blackjack vines and briars. Briars were still lodged in my face and hands. I was filthy. My hands and teeth were stained from the berries. My lips, tongue, and hands were literally blue. My appearance was bad, but I had survived it. I was alive.

I took a bath, the first soap and shampoo bath that I had taken in 56 days. It was almost as good as that barbecued chicken, maybe better. I brushed my teeth. My lips and hands were still stained, but I was clean.

I searched the house and found a fresh set of clothes. They were very loose fitting; I was really thin. I also found a pair of Indian moccasins. I put them on. They fit well and were quiet. I wanted to be as quiet as possible; I was still plenty scared. I found a $100 bill in my mother's dresser and took it. I found a bottle of vodka in the kitchen and fixed a drink to calm me. I was completely nervous; the adrenaline had been flowing since early morning when I first came out of the woods. That drink calmed me a little, so I mixed another one. I wanted to get high. I searched the house again. I thought that my mother might have a joint stashed somewhere. I couldn't find one. I mixed another drink. Where can I get a joint?

I continued to drink. Surely there must be some weed in this house. But where? And then it dawned on me. The attic. I stored pounds and pounds of marijuana in the attic during high school, certainly there would be some up there. I searched the attic, and sure enough, I was able to scrape up enough dope for a couple of joints. I got high.

I contemplated my next move. I should probably take the vodka and hit the woods again. No, my body is much too weak. I need to get out of town! I have the money I stole I could take the bus. Wait. Someone is at the door. It was my mother. She walked into the kitchen.

"Hey!"

"Who are you? What are you doing here?" She was startled.

"Mom, it's me. Ricky!"

"Well, I'm glad you told me. Ricky, you look awful! Where have you been? How did you get in this house?"

I did look awful. I was high, drunk, scared, and weak. My mother was terribly afraid of me. The word around town was that I was armed and dangerous. I could look at her and tell that she was afraid.

" I told you not to come here."

"Mom, I need your help. I've got to get out of here."

"Why me, Lord?"

"Mom, you've got to help me."

She didn't have a choice. She had to help me; she had to get me out of her house. We began discussing my options. She suggested that I go to Seattle, Washington. Her sister lived there. We started making plans: she would drive me to another town and put me on a bus. It was all set. We would leave at dark.

As we sat talking, my mother's boyfriend walked in. George was not my favorite person. In fact, I couldn't stand him. He didn't like me very much either. I had beaten him up on several occasions. He would never take my Dad's place. George had learned not to mess with me.

"Oh my God! Ricky? Is that you?"

"Of course it's me. Now shut your mouth! I don't want to hear a word out of you."

George was plenty scared! I heard that my picture was on flyers posted all around town. My name was the current news "Ricky Sinclair, armed and dangerous." George was afraid. My mother was afraid. They wanted me out of their house.

I never had a killing instinct in my whole life. I thank God for that. If I had one, it would have surfaced then. I felt like a hunted animal. My own family was afraid of me. It was truly me against the world. I couldn't even trust my own family. I wasn't armed, except for that old cat food can top. I wasn't dangerous to the point of killing, but I was desperate.

George soon ran out of cigarettes. He told my mother that he was going to run to the store and get another pack.

"No!" I exclaimed. "No one leaves this house until I'm out of town."

George pleaded, "Please Ricky. I really need some cigarettes."

For some reason-I'm not sure why-I decided to let him go.

"OK! To the store and right back. Five minutes. Do you understand?"

"Yeah! Thanks Ricky."

He was gone for what seemed to be an eternity. The minutes ticked by. I knew I shouldn't have trusted him. What was he doing?

Finally, after about 30 minutes, he returned. And right behind him, a swat team. No, it couldn't be. I had been through so much. I was almost free! But there they were, squad cars screaming in, with George right up front. Within seconds the house was completely surrounded. I could see them from every window: men in camouflage with M16 rifles, men with shotguns, state police, local police, and George. Did George rat on me? Who cares? It doesn't matter now. What can I do to escape?

They yelled with a megaphone, "OK! We know you're in there! We've got you surrounded! Come out with your hands up!"

I ran through the house. Where can I hide? They'll be crashing through the door any minute! I tried to climb into the dryer. I was too large. Where? I ran into the hall, reached up, pulled the attic door down, and then yelled at my mother.

"Close this door behind me!"

She did. The attic was dark. I crawled over to a corner and hid. The police crashed through the front door. The search was on.

"We know you're in here! We'll find you!"

They searched the house for about 20 minutes. They knew I was there. Finally, from the hall, one of them yelled, "Up there!"

My luck had just run out. I was terrified. The attic door opened, and the light from the hall began shining into the darkness. Then came the sound of that brave cop on those steps. It must have taken plenty of guts to climb into that dark attic to get me. He knew that I was up there. What if I had a gun? He didn't know that I was unarmed. That's guts. Within minutes his flashlight was shining in my face.

"I see you! Come on out. Don't try anything foolish!"

He handcuffed me. I was at the end of my rope. They were very upset with me, and with good reason; I had really put them through it.

Looking Back

The 56-day reprieve had ended. That horrible escapade had only postponed my inevitable destination -prison. The final page of the story of the notorious Ricky Sinclair was forever etched in stone. My future was vanishing right before my eyes. The officers pulled me out of the attic, applied handcuffs and leg irons, and gave me a free, taxpayer ride to the parish jail.

I was escorted into the jail. They added simple escape to my charges. They took finger prints and mugshots; my appearance had changed plenty. Finally, they took me to a cell, the drunk tank. The detox cell was in plain view of the jailer. It had a glass wall through which the inmate could be watched for alcohol or drug withdrawal problems. The detox cell became my home. I was caged like an animal. The lights stayed on around the clock. They wanted to be able to see me at all times. I wasn't going anywhere.

During those first few days, I began to realize that there was something wrong with me. There was something really wrong. I wasn't like most people. My idea of life was a can of beer and a half-naked woman playing volleyball. Life was a party, nothing else. And now, at age 22, my life was over. It was really over, no second chances. Everybody knows that 3 felony convictions, all drug-related, means life in prison. I would never see another beer or any women playing volleyball. I would never see another day outside of jail.

How much time would the escape charges add to the 80 year sentence facing me? Who cares? It doesn't matter. I'm just different. It's me. It has to be me. The police, the narcotics agents, and the judges can't all be wrong. I'm the one that's wrong. I deserve a life in prison.

I began to search the depths of my soul for answers. How could this be possible? Where had I gone wrong? I had started out as such a good kid. I came from a good family. My life had only been one of fun. I hadn't hurt anyone.

I could remember passing by a state prison as a child out riding with my dad. I must have been five or six years old. We talked about the inmates. I remember telling my dad that those gators out there must be some kind of bad. Now, 17 years later, I was on my way to being one of those bad gators. It was my worst nightmare, and it had come true. I kept thinking back over my life.

I really had a strange childhood. At age seven I developed spinal meningitis. It's a rare disease that normally leaves its victims either dead or severely brain damaged. I was in the hospital for a long time. I had fever over 105 for many days; I almost died. I took spinal tap treatments to remove fluid from my spinal column. It was a painful ordeal, but I managed to survive. Many people lose hearing from the high fevers, but I didn't. I came through it without any permanent damage.

I had my appendix taken out at age seven and my tonsils removed at age eight. I contracted spinal meningitis again at age twelve. The doctors were perplexed that I had gotten it again. They told my parents that the odds of getting that disease twice were comparable to being struck by lightening twice. I went through the spinal tap procedures again. Fortunately, I was able to survive it again without any lasting effects. To pull through spinal meningitis at any one time is truly a miracle, but to have gotten it twice and to have survived both times without any permanent damage was simply astonishing.

My dad played music as a hobby during my childhood. He would take our entire family with him to parties to watch him play. I began sneaking beer out of other people's ice chests at the age of nine. It seemed to be the "grown-up" thing to do.

My dad caught me; he was mad. He didn't want me to drink, but I kept sneaking around doing it anyway. Surely I was old enough to drink. Besides, they did it.

My parents were both good-hearted people. They were well respected in our community. We were members of the local Catholic church, though we didn't go regularly. We were wealthy. My dad owned a successful meat packaging company, 1,900 acres of farm land, and 600 head of cattle. We owned bulldozers, 18-wheelers, airplanes, cars, and plenty of money. My parents were the type of people that would help others, and they had lots of friends. They took legal custody of several of my friends, kids who were the children of several of their friends. These kids grew up in our home. I really loved my parents, and I wanted to be just like my dad.

Both of my parents were afflicted with a dreadful problem -alcoholism. I can't remember a single day that my parents didn't drink at least a fifth of whiskey. The drinking really had a hold on both of them. I guess that's why they were so against our drinking. They were also against drugs. My dad told me to turn in anyone that I caught using dope. He said if anyone pushed dope on me, that I was to knock them out and drag them to the principal's office.

My dad had good morals, but I'm afraid that the power of money must have gone to his head. When I was around twelve, he got drunk and made a statement that he was god. He said that nobody could take him down. He bragged about his company, his land, and his money. I'll never forget it; he just seemed to believe that he was invincible. Six months later, he developed cancer. The doctors gave him less than a year to live.

During my dad's sickness, he began to vomit profusely. The cancer was taking its toll. One of his buddies was a doper and suggested that dad try marijuana to relieve the vomiting problem. He did. Then one day, I walked in and caught him getting high. It was a confusing moment. There he was getting high, and he had instructed me to turn in anyone that I caught doing that. I was thirteen. I asked him what he was doing, and he explained. He told me that he had just started smoking it, and that it wasn't that bad. He let me try it. We got high. It was my first time.

At fourteen I was getting into anything and everything, everything but school work. Dad's condition had declined. He was taking lots of radiation treatments, so he gave me the bulk of his responsibilities around the house. He lay in bed for a year taking thorazine. I would usually be the one to give him the thorazine shots. His condition improved, and soon he tried to take over the house again. I became rebellious; I liked the responsibilities and didn't want to start minding him again, so problems developed between us. We started fist fighting and other crazy stuff like that. Things were never the same. I had once worshipped my dad, but after the fighting, we never really got to be close again.

I really had a rough time of it at age fourteen. During that year we lost about $2 million. I contracted hepatitis. Later that same year, I totaled out my mother's Mazda. It was a bad wreck. A friend and I were riding around smoking pot and throwing bottle rockets out of the window. One of the rockets hit the door, ricocheted into the back seat, and went off. Startled, I let go of the steering wheel and turned around to look, losing control of the car. We hit a tree, turned three flips, jumped a fence, and landed sideways in a field. We were taken to the hospital. I underwent surgery twice on my elbow. As you can see, I was no stranger to the hospital.

At fifteen I wrecked my pickup truck while coming home from a bar one night. I left the truck, along with a bag of dope which I had forgotten about, and caught a ride home. The next morning, a state highway patrolman came to my house. I was still asleep. He talked with my dad about my condition. This was during the time that I was rebelling against Dad. They decided to try to teach me a lesson, so the patrolman came into my room and woke me up. He pulled me out of my bed, handcuffed me, drug me out of the house, and put me in the back of the squad car. I begged him to let me put some pants on; I was still in my underwear. He told me that I wouldn't need any pants where I was going. Dad thought the whole thing was hilarious, but it didn't help me a bit.

Looking back, it's amazing that I'm alive. I have probably been through at least seven or eight major car accidents. Why am I still alive?

I always hung out with guys that were older than me. Most of my friends were at least three or four years older than I was. They were into things that kids my age didn't do, like heavy drugs. One of those guys was really into cocaine. He was the first one to ever stick a needle in my arm. I was about fifteen. I had taken lots of pills and stuff, but the needle is like crossing a line. I had been doing Quaaludes, valiums, and speed since age thirteen, but I crossed the line into intravenous drugs at age fifteen.

At that point, the drug thing was really on. I did it all: cocaine, tulenol, seconal, morphine, Demerol, delaudid, heroin, meth-amphetamine, acid, and mushrooms. I smoked Sherman, cigars dipped in formaldehyde. I did it all. I continuously smoked marijuana. I didn't even count smoking pot as getting high. I smoked pot like most people smoked cigarettes. I smoked it all day, everyday. I wasn't completely dressed if I didn't have at least a half an ounce of pot on me.

I was a dealer, a walking drug store. If I didn't have it, I could get it fast. I started out selling weed stolen from my dad, then began ordering speed out of the trucker magazines. You could buy 1000 hits of caffeine for $20; they looked just like black mollies. I would sell them for one dollar each. I sold LSD, pot, Quaaludes, cocaine, everything.

I remember selling some Roach 2's to some kids in high school. It was a powerful drug that was used by the guerrillas in El Salvador during war. It works as both an upper and a downer: with adrenaline flowing it's an upper, otherwise it's a downer. It was to be broken into quarters. I told those kids that, but they didn't listen. They each took an entire hit. It really tore them up. At lunch, they couldn't even hit their mouth with a chicken leg. I was worried. Luckily, they were too wasted to tell the principal where they had gotten it. It was a close call; I had plenty of it on me.

During those years, I sold drugs that I couldn't even pronounce. I learned the name of some of those drugs from the police and the judges. I was really out there. What happened? I wasn't born a dealer, a drug addict, or smuggler. I was born a baby, but through situations in life, I had gradually become these things.

My life was a mess. One time, I went to Pensacola, Florida, on a chartered airplane with a friend's dad. We tore the town down. Coming back, he and I were both broke. We rode home, from Pensacola to Baton Rouge, in a taxi cab. Another time, I flew to Los Angeles, partied on the beach, and flew back the same day, a trip of less than 24 hours. I was a real knucklehead.

During high school, there were plenty of times that I stayed up all night shooting dope. I would get my buddies, dopers who were 35 to 40 years old, to drop me off the next morning at school. It made school rough. I would go there high and looking bad: no sleep, bath, or clean clothes. Everyone knew. During second hour, I would be coming down, "Jonesing," and would fall asleep in class. It was bad. Then, after school, we had football practice. How did I make it?

My football coach really liked me; I was good. I scored 26 touchdowns in one season. I would score two or three touchdowns during the first half, then they would sit me on the bench during the second half to keep from running up the score. They gave my dad a trophy for bringing me to practice. I lettered every year that I played. If it weren't for drugs, I could have really gone somewhere in football. I was out my sophomore year with "car-wreck" elbow, the Mazda wreck. I came back my junior year, but the drugs were really bringing me down. Everyone knew it; the football coach would check my arm for needle tracks at practice. I was bad news.

I missed 60 days straight during my senior year; I didn't even attempt football. I would rather do drugs than play ball. Drugs were my life. I missed many days of school out partying. My uncle, a medical doctor, wrote me a doctor's excuse for two months. That excuse was vital to my graduation. All in all, I must have missed 80 days of school my senior year.

It was during my senior year that I got busted with my first felony conviction. A so-called friend of mine ratted on me. He set me up. I sold some valium, marijuana, and cocaine to several undercover narcotics agents, and they busted me. The judge allowed me to finish my senior year before requiring me to serve out my sentence.

I was seventeen and my attitude deteriorated from its normal lousy state. I was looking at jail time at graduation, and it really had me bummed out. I went crazy with the drugs. Right after graduation, I pulled up 300 units of morphine in a rig and rammed it home. It was three times the dosage I normally did. It was my first overdose - the first OD, I just went out, that's all I remember. When I came back, I started looking for another hit. I didn't care; I was looking at jail time.

Soon after graduation, I went to jail. They put me in the same cell with the guy that had set me up, and we fought. I nearly beat him half to death before they could break us up. It didn't help matters at all. I was moved to a cell by myself. During my jail term, there were very few visitors. Where were all of my buddies now? My aunt from Texas, who had been praying several years for me, sent me a Bible. I never even opened it. Jesus was far from my mind.

My dad died while I was in prison. He was 44 years old. I had served over eight months, so they reduced my sentence to time served and let me out to attend the funeral. I went to the funeral, and then it was back to the drugs.

I was a junky, a bad junky. I wouldn't sit down with less than an eight ball of cocaine. Less than that wouldn't be worth coming down over. I was the type of junky that would take a big hit of free-based cocaine, hold it, then stick a needle in my arm at the same time. I would do drugs until either someone went to the hospital or we ran out. I was a fool, a nut.

At eighteen, I picked up a 28 gram rock in Houston. A buddy and I stayed in the bathroom for three days shooting it. We broke out the big spoon. That was some powerful coke. On the third day, they took my buddy to the hospital. He had been straining so hard that he developed a strangulated hernia. He lost a testicle. I never left the bathroom. I kept on shooting it, alone now.

That afternoon, another friend stopped by. He was a Vietnam veteran who was once hooked on 11 grams of heroin per day. I loaded the big spoon up with cocaine, then drew up 70 units. It was pure yellow cocaine. I offered it to my buddy. I told him that it was the best hit that anyone had ever offered him, or ever would. He started shaking, but managed to turn it down. So I did it. I did the whole spoon. It was my second overdose. I just went out. That's all I remember about it. When I woke up, my chest was pounding and my mouth was bleeding. I wanted another hit.

"No way man!" my wife cried. "You just nearly died!" They had kept me from swallowing my tongue. I was a very sick man.

While sitting in the cell looking back over my life, I realized that it was simply a miracle that I was even alive. There was no other explanation. I had been through so much: I had overdosed three times, taken lots of drugs, come close to death many times, and had stared down the wrong end of several guns. I had even been kidnapped. Surely my being alive was a miracle.

Drugs and Guns

Artie was an ornery, tough guy. We had fought once before. We had been doing mandrax. He had gotten mad, had grabbed a crescent wrench, and had beaten me in the head with it. I had grabbed him around the neck and wouldn't let go. The blood had poured from the back of my head. When he finally quit hitting me, I ran home to get a gun. It was a 1/2 mile journey through the woods. I made it quick, I wanted revenge, bad.

I made it home, but Jeannie wouldn't let me have the gun. She had it hidden. I searched the house, but was unable to find it, so I grabbed a stick and headed back toward Artie's house. It was dark now. I ran through the woods. My body was extremely weak from a combination of the mandrax, alcohol, and blood loss.

When I got there, the cops were everywhere. Artie's wife had called the police. I waited in the woods for a minute, but they didn't leave. I couldn't attack him with the police there, so I walked back home. Jeannie was worried; my head was still bleeding. I had lost about a pint of blood.

Jeannie insisted that I go to the hospital. I was dizzy. I knew she was right, so we went. The nurses wanted to take a urine specimen, but I refused. I was wasted, and they knew it. They wouldn't admit me. We went to two other hospitals, but I wouldn't cooperate there either. Finally, Jeannie gave up, and we went back home. I was a hardheaded dude -both figuratively and literally. Later, Artie and I made up; after all, we had only been playing.

Several years later, Mike, one of my smuggling buddies, came by my house with an eight ball of cocaine. He asked me a silly question, "You wanna do some coke?"

"Sure! What you got?"

He told me that it was a good eight ball, $3^1/_2$ grams. I suggested that we go over to my brother's trailer; nobody would be there. Looking back on it, I think that Mike was there to set me up. Something was really strange about the whole thing, the way it went down. Mike was in trouble with the law, and after that night he did some "funny" things. Anyway, we went to my brother's house and broke out a rig. An eight ball was enough to last me about an hour. We got high.

I didn't know it right then, but the house was surrounded by a surveillance team. I'm sure that they had come there to bust me with his coke. They must have been planning to bust the door down and catch me with it, but they waited too long. I had already finished it. It was all gone. After doing the coke, Artie showed up. We continued to party.

It's hard to say what set Artie off that night, but something did. We started yelling at each other, and soon the fists were flying again. We fought from the living room to the front yard. We fought down the driveway. He was really mad; I didn't realize how mad. He went to his car and donned a holster belt and pistol.

I could hear him screaming something about killing me. He got in his car. I stood in the driveway, pointed my finger at him, and yelled, "You big sissy, put your gun up. I won't hurt you." He yelled something, so I walked over to his car.

We weren't playing this time. He picked up a shotgun, aimed it at my chest, and pulled the trigger. Click. It didn't go off. Immediately, he drew for the pistol, and it did go off. He shot himself in the leg. It was quite a moment. That's when I saw the surveillance police. They dashed up from the woods with their guns pulled. They startled me as much as the gun shot did. Artie was rolling around on the ground in obvious pain.

One of the cops picked up the shotgun and ejected the shell. He yelled out to a buddy, "Hey, come look at this!"

"What?"

"This shotgun. The firing pin hit the shell. It's a miracle that it didn't go off!"

Yes, it was truly a miracle that I lived through that night.

I've really dealt a bunch of pot over the years. Mexican guerrillas were always hanging around my house. They were expendable people, dopers that the big-timers had left to watch us, the ones with their fronted dope. Nobody cared whether these guys got busted or not. Most of them didn't care either. I guess none of us did. The police knew we were dealing; it was just a matter of time until they would bust us.

I remember going up to Indiana one winter. Some of the Mexicans hanging around my house had a connection up there who had more pot than he could sell. They asked me to go up there, get some of it, and bring it back here to sell on a front. So I did. I stole my mother's car and headed north. I headed out of Louisiana at midnight wearing short pants and a pair of flip flops. I hit the first snow of the year in Illinois. The roads were iced over. I pulled into a self-service gas station and skidded up to the pumps. It was well below zero. I jumped out of the car, wearing shorts and flip flops, to fill up. Everyone was wearing gloves and parkas. They stared as if to say, "Who is this nut?"

I picked up the thirty pounds in Indiana and returned home. It turned out to be a bad deal; the Mexicans wanted too much for it. They ticked me off, so I stole it. I hid the whole lot under my mother's house. Now they were ticked off. They confronted me, "Where's our pot?"

"How should I know? I thought ya'll put it in the barn!"

They thought that I had it but couldn't be sure. They were mad; they wanted their pot. I continued to lie -they'd never get the truth out of me. Finally, they began a diligent search. That pot was worth $30,000 and they were determined to find it. They looked everywhere.

Later that day, the sky darkened, and thenrain poured. I was afraid that the weed was going to get wet; a stream of rainwater was flowing under the house. The Mexicans were still searching, so I had to hurry. The weed had to come out from underneath the house. I laid some newspaper down in the attic, then hurried the pot up there. Mom asked what I was doing. I threw her a pound.

"Don't worry about it! Just keep your mouth shut!" The pot was soaked. Water began dripping through the kitchen ceiling, and Mom's boyfriend wanted to know what was going on.

"George," I explained, "stay out of the attic! I've got some weed up there. It's wet. I'm letting it dry out. Just keep your mouth shut! The Mexicans are looking for it and if they find it, we're all dead!"

George freaked out. He got a hammer and nailed all of the windows in the house shut. We were all afraid, with good reason. The Mexicans had called in some hired killers. They wanted their money. They threatened me at gun point; they threatened my family. They made it perfectly clear, "We want the money! The money! The money! The money! You're all dead if we don't get the money!"

"I don't have your dope or your money!" I pleaded.

They weren't satisfied. "Borrow it!" they demanded.

They escorted my cousin and me to the local bank. We tried to take out a loan, but were turned down. Luckily, the Mexicans were satisfied that we had tried. They decided to let us live. We were instructed that this was never to happen again. Ever! I left that dope in the attic for a long time. It was a close call!

Kidnapped

By the age of fifteen, the dealing was on, wide open. It took plenty of money to support my habit. I was a full-fledged dealer-growing, selling, and smuggling pot. Normally, I only smuggled marijuana, thinking that the sentence would be easier if I got busted. I occasionally smuggled Roche-2's and pasadrene, Mexican valium.

I went to Florida, Texas, and Mexico. I was always going somewhere. Florida and Texas were easy, as drug smuggling goes, but Mexico was a totally different animal; you're no longer under United States jurisdiction. You can be killed in Mexico, and no one back home would ever know. And if you wind up in Mexican prison, well that's really bad. You'll need family to bring you food, or you'll go hungry.

I've smuggled with many different people, both friends and relatives. I've smuggled with the best. We've done it many different ways. Sometimes, we'd swim bails across the Rio Grande River at night. We'd wrap the bails in plastic and have Mexicans swim them across.

They'd have a bail under each arm. Other times, we'd rent a U-haul truck and drive six or seven hundred pounds of pot across the border. You could make a ton of money, $300 per pound, but; it was highly risky. We'd wait for a storm, a flooding rain, then just drive through. The adrenaline would really be going. We would sell large quantities in Texas, right over the border.' We had money running out of our ears.

We usually dealt directly with the Mexican police. They would smuggle it for us. We'd go into Mexico, meet with them, examine the pot, and then return to Texas. They would load it on large produce trucks and drive it across the border. We'd take possession in Texas, then return to Louisiana to sell it. They would send a guerrilla with us to protect their interest, the fronted dope. I've been into Mexico many times, but always preferred partying in McAllen, Texas while someone else drove across the border.

The method of smuggling always depended upon whom you were dealing with and the connections they had. There were many different ways of doing it. I'd normally bring 100 pounds back to Louisiana, sell it over a period of about 10 days, then go back. I primarily bought cocaine in Texas or Florida, and sometimes Louisiana. We were big-time. I'd make $10,000 in 10 days.

Smuggling is like playing with a rattlesnake. The question is not whether or not he'll bite, but when. There's a certain rush that goes with smuggling; I'd get that rush just thinking about it. It's probably similar to the rush that a gambler gets at a casino. It's a demonic thing.

I stored pounds of weed in the attic of my parent's home. You'd never catch me without pot. During the "Day of Rock and Roll" concert, I rolled a quarter pound of weed into one joint and took it to the Super Dome. A security guard searched my football satchel at the gate. He put his hands right on that big joint. I was tense. I was prepared to hit him in the mouth and run. He knew it. He let us go.

We went to our seats with that big doobie. I cut a coke can in half and shoved it up on one end for a mouthpiece. It took 17 lighters to light it. We passed it around, and everybody got high. I was the center of attention, the guy with the big joint. I was always blowing money like that, either mine or someone else's.

My cousin, Danny, and I had set up shop in Covington. We had been working with two Mexicans, Peppie and Louis, for a long time and were doing well. We had sold a lot of pot for them, and they were beginning to trust us. One time they brought in a 150 pound lot, some good dope. They needed to get back to Mexico, so they left us with the 150 pounds on a front; there was no sitter. That pot was worth a bundle, a 150 grand.

They were gone nearly three weeks, a long time for us to be left alone. We sold most of the pot, but we didn't have the money. We had blown it doing drugs, drinking expensive liquor, and eating expensive meals. We had free-based a bunch of coke. We were short, forty thousand dollars short.

One morning Peppie and Louis showed up. They wanted their money, all of it. We had a good story prepared for them: "Guys, we got busted. Dusty's dad found 40 pounds and burned it. There was nothing we could do!"

They were hot, "You lie! You lie! You lie! You do cocaine! You free-base all our money!" They pulled their guns, "Let's go! Let's go! Come now! Get in car! We take a little ride!"

They drove us across the Causeway. "Ha! Ha! Ha! You crab bait!"

I knew they were serious. They had kidnapped us and were surely going to kill us. We were petrified. I just knew that they were going to stop any minute, shoot us, and throw our bodies over the side of the bridge. My mind was racing. What can I do? I had to say something. "Peppie," I nervously mumbled. "We didn't free-base your money. We told you the truth. I'm serious!"

"Right! You dead, crab bait!"

"We're no good to you dead! Look, if you let us live, we can make you some money, big money!"

"Sure dead man."

"Look Peppie, I know a guy that makes crystal meth. He's got a lab and everything."

"Where?" he asked.

"West Feliciana! I can hook you up with him! With your connections, you could make some big money!" I knew this would be enticing to Peppie. It had to be. It was our only chance.

"How you know this guy?" he questioned.

"He's an old friend. We go way back. I know him well. He's been looking to move!" I pleaded.

"OK! We make deal! Get your guy. Move lab Denver, Colorado. One more thing. You move it! Personally! Things go smoothly, you live. If not, crab bait!"

I knew two guys that had a methamphetamine lab in West Feliciana. They had recently blown up a house making the stuff, and the heat was really on them, big time. I felt confident that they would go for this deal; they needed to move. It would work great for them. After all, I was the one that was going to have to smuggle the lab to Denver.

Peppie and Louis called in Pete, a hired killer from Mexico. He was hired to make sure that Danny and I moved the lab. I hooked Peppie and Louis up with the guys in West Feliciana. Fortunately, they went for it. We made the deal, it was all set. The only thing left to do was to smuggle that lab to Denver.

Pete was a nervous little guy who seemed to enjoy his work. He was constantly waiving his gun around. He made me nervous-he made us all nervous.

I explained to him how I felt, "Pete, if anyone winds up missing around here, it's gonna be me and you. You need to understand that. I'm not playing. Mess up and you'll never make it out of these woods. We're gonna keep our end of the deal with Peppie and Louis, so you keep that pistol holstered. Understand!"

Pete just laughed, "I've got a 55 gallon drum of hydrochloric acid. Your bones will be gone in 3 days."

I laughed. He had understood me; that was easy to see. Peppie had warned him about me. I was nobody to play with, and he knew it. We didn't have any trouble out of him.

The big day finally came. It was time to move the lab. We disassembled it, put it in two cars, and headed out. It was a nasty thing: the magnesium stirrers, the SAPA metha-ketone chemicals, the two way flasks, and a lot of other smelly stuff. It stunk bad, but at least we had escaped the "crab bait" scene. It was a long trip from south Louisiana to Denver, Colorado, a two day trip. Pete led the way, and Danny and I followed with the lab. We were each in a separate vehicle. Pete had instructed us to stay behind him so we did.

It was a smooth trip. The only close call was in Kansas. We were on a long, straight, flat highway. You could literally see for miles. Up ahead, I could see the blue lights. Oh no, it's a road block. I was terribly frightened. I knew that Pete would kill anybody that got in our way. It was—nauseating. What can I do? How can I stop him? The tension was really building up inside me. As we got closer I could tell that it wasn't a road block; oh thank goodness, it was only a stalled vehicle.

Denver was a pleasant sight. We had made it and were going to live. We delivered the lab to Louis and Peppie, but they didn't let us go. We had to hang around as collateral to make sure that everything worked out between them and our guy. It took three weeks to get the lab up and running. We worked with their chemist, and Pete hung around to keep an eye on us. Finally, after about a month, they let us go.

Prisoner Set Free

But now it was June 1987, and I was a jailed drug dealer. I had been back to magistrate court and they had scheduled my court appearance for late October. I was living in a cell block, lockdown. There was no way out, no chance of escape. The sheriff had instructed the jailers that I wasn't to leave the cell without handcuffs and leg irons. Occasionally, they'd let us go outside to play basketball. It's a tough game in handcuffs; it's tough to run in leg irons.

One day while sitting in my cell, thinking back over the past, Officer James came in to see me. He was the jailer on duty during my escape. I knew that he'd really been through the ringer over that. How could he even stand to see me?

He told me that he just wanted to deliver something that my mother had dropped off. It was the big Catholic Bible that my aunt had sent me during my first jail term. It was dusty; I had never opened it. Officer James told me that I should read it. He ministered to me and told me that I needed Jesus.

I was facing a life term in prison. It was frightening, but Officer James encouraged me.

"Ricky, you'll be fine. You've got everything! You've got Jesus!" He knew that what I had was real.

I kept seeking God through His word, the Bible. I read it all the time. I wanted to know more about Him. I wanted to please Him. Most of the police around the jail thought that I was faking, but I wasn't. I told the sheriff that God had saved me and that He had called me to preach. He laughed, "Ha! Ha! Ha! Sure Ricky! That's just great."

I went to court in late October. The judge sentenced me to seven years of hard labor at the Louisiana State Penitentiary in Angola, Louisiana. It's the largest prison in Louisiana. The charges in New Orleans would come later. I was sure that Angola would be my home for the rest of my time on planet Earth. My knees shook as he read the sentence; I was engulfed with fear.

I remained in West Feliciana Parish jail for several more weeks, and Officer James continued ministering. He was God sent. He helped prepare me for prison.

Inevitably, the big day came. I was transported to Hunt Correctional Institute, ARDC, for inmate evaluation and processing. It was really tough. The guards harassed us, trying to provoke us to retaliation. It was part of the classification process. They were testing us. The ARDC authorities decided that I shouldn't go to Angola. I had grown up near there and knew some of the guards. Some of them had chased me during the escape. They were mad at me. Angola was inappropriate; it would not be my home.

They decided to send me to Washington Correctional Institute (WCI) near Bogalusa, Louisiana. I stayed at Hunt Correctional for about two weeks and then was sent on to WCI, the second largest prison in Louisiana, to begin the sentence.

A majority of the felonry at WCI was black. They ran the prison. I was a young, small, white boy, and they tested me. During the first day there, while taking a shower, a large black man told me that I had nothing to worry about. He said, "Boy, you're mine. You're the one for me. I'm gonna be your man. I'm gonna take real good care of you."

I told him quick, "I'm my own man. I'm not for anybody. I can take care of myself. Don't mess with me!"

He was staring at my naked body there in that shower. It was sickening. It was the first of many days that I'd have to defend myself. Homosexuality was prevalent in prison; it was everywhere. I never got used to seeing it; it was always nauseating. I let everybody know that I was a Christian, that I was not a homosexual, and that I could fight if I had to. I went to prison a man, was a man while there, and came out a man. I never had to fight even once, thank God.

I learned right away that I needed some different underwear. The briefs, or "catch-me's" as they're referred to in prison, had to go. That's what had caused that first confrontation. I called my grandmother and told her to bring me some boxer shorts immediately. I never liked boxers, but I wore them for four years. I didn't want to give anybody the wrong idea, no sense starting trouble.

There were inmate gangs in prison, and they were always trying to set me up. I was considered a rich convict; my grandmother was sending me money. Some of the gang members would catch me coming out of the canteen, the inmate store, and tell me to buy them some sugar and coffee. They told me that if I would buy it, no one would mess with me. I refused, and they didn't like it. "We're gonna get you!" they'd threaten. I stood my ground and never bought them anything. Finally, the harassment waned and eventually ceased.

The first 90 days of prison were tough. I worked in the field all day digging up stumps. The guards would wake us up 4:00 a.m. Breakfast was at 5:30, roll call at 7:00. Every day! We were herded through the guard line at 7:00 by guards on horseback. They were armed with shotguns. They'd make sure everyone was present, then lead us into the field to dig. We'd dig with picks and shovels. There were few breaks, and sometimes the tempers would flare. I've seen inmates hit other inmates in the head with their shovel. Some of them were hurt really bad. I heard that an inmate had been killed in the field a few months prior. There were several inmates killed in a cell block during my incarceration. Prison is like being caged up with a bunch of animals. It's no fun.

Right away, I got involved with the prison church, the Victory Faith Fellowship. The church was run by inmates. We had an inmate pastor, inmate deacons, elders, an inmate choir, everything. It was a great church; everyone was filled with the Holy Ghost! We met three nights per week from six to nine o'clock. We praised the Lord with song, studied the Bible, and there was even preaching. It was great. That church laid the foundation of the faith that I stand on today.

The inmate pastor, Brother Robert Early, was a powerful man of God. He had been in prison for 12 years for bank robbery and had been saved in prison. He is out of prison today and is still serving God. I was blessed to have him as my pastor. He water baptized me in a cattle trough at WCI during December 1987. It was a cold experience, but well worth it! Brother Early was a walking Bible, as were many of the Christian inmates. I had some great brothers in prison and stay in touch with most of them to this day. Many have gotten out of prison and have entered the ministry. It's great to hear from them.

I backslid one time during my first few weeks in prison; I smoked a joint with a guy there. We got high, but it just wasn't the same. It just wasn't me anymore. I felt so guilty and begged God to forgive me. I must have repented at least 3,000 times.

God spoke to me during that time. He told me that I was at a cross road-to choose whom I was going to serve. He told me that if I chose sin, I would never see my family again. I would never see another day outside of prison. He went on to say, that if I chose to serve Him, He would get me out of prison. He reminded me that He was running the universe, that He could do anything. He said that my life would be good. I chose God and haven't backslid since. I'm right with God, I'm committed to Jesus, forever.

The biggest concern that I had during those first years was my wife, Jeannie. She wasn't saved. I had witnessed to her, had prayed for her, and had asked some of the other convicts to pray for her. I had written many long letters to her, but she just wasn't receptive. I didn't know what else to do. I was afraid she thought I was faking the whole thing. I felt responsible. She was a good girl; I was the one that had led her astray. I wanted to win her to the Lord more than anything.

There are steps every convict has to go through in prison. The first 90 days is spent in the field, digging, as I mentioned. Everybody goes through that. During the next 90 days, you're assigned to a particular job. Then you go before a board which assigns you to a specific rehabilitation program, a vocational school. You learn a trade to use when you re-enter society.

I spent my second 90 days in the kitchen washing dishes. I'd have to be there every morning at 4:30 a.m. It was a good job. After this second phase, I entered a vocational training course, automobile body and fender repair. I graduated just days before my parole.

My living quarters in prison consisted of a bunk bed and wall locker in a 120-bed dormitory. It was a rough environment, no privacy at all. All of the toilets and sinks were made of stainless steel. There were no partitions between toilets, no stalls. There were no secrets in prison. Everybody knew everything about everybody.

Sometimes there would be guards watching you sit on the commode, and some of those guards were females. It was simply humiliating.

Prison is not a good life. Sometimes I would go to the bathroom in the middle of the night and walk in on two homosexuals in the act. The only thing you could do would be to go back to your bunk. You couldn't even use the bathroom. It was quite inconvenient. During the day you could only use the bathroom at designated times. I hated that. All in all, prison is hell.

Prison was a sinful environment: cussing, fighting, gambling, drugs, and homosexuality. The dormitory stunk. You could often smell marijuana. I believe there are as many drugs in prison as there are on the streets. I steered clear of all that and stayed to myself. I'd sit on my bunk and read the Bible. There was always a lot of yelling and loud talk in the dormitory: inmates fighting in the recreation room over television channels; inmates fighting over homosexual lovers and drugs. They could find all kinds of reasons to fight. It was like living in a zoo.

But the worst thing about prison was the loneliness. It was worse than the threats, the fighting, the prison chow, the lack of privacy, the ever-present homosexuality, and the loud talk. I missed my wife. I missed my son. Loneliness can dominate your entire life in prison. It can destroy you.

I stayed faithful to God through prison. I took Bible correspondence courses from schools all around the country, prayed for fellow inmates, and cast demons out of inmates on the cell block floor. I had my trust in God and had high hopes for the future. God was going to get me out of prison. He had promised; I knew He would come through!

The best news of my life came during the second year of prison. I called home to learn that Jeannie had been saved. She was really saved! A giant weight had been lifted off of my shoulders. I praised God.

I thanked my brothers who had prayed. I was elated! Things were looking up.

Near the end of my third year, the St. Bernard Parish court sent orders scheduling my appearance for trial. They would seal my fate, my destiny. I had been praying about it for three years, and had hoped that they might even forget about it, but no chance. The anxiety grew as the date approached. I asked everybody to pray. I reminded God daily that He had promised my freedom; I had held my end of the bargain. My grandmother hired me a good lawyer. He would do all that he could.

The court date finally arrived. I was taken to New Orleans. It was my first time to leave WCI in over three years. I prayed on the drive. God reminded me that He was faithful. I was optimistic; they would surely set me free!

The guards escorted me into the courtroom. I was wearing an orange prison suit, a big minus. I stood beside my lawyer. The charges were read: "The State of Louisiana versus Ricky James Sinclair, alias Kent Douglas Smith, alias James Louis Winnfield. One count possession of marijuana with intent to distribute, 14 pounds. One count possession of ecstasy, with intent to distribute, one ounce." I was relatively calm under the circumstances. The court proceeded.

Finally, the judge read my sentence: "I've reviewed your file. This is your third felony conviction. Every thing says that you're a habitual criminal, that you can't change. I don't know why I'm doing this, but I'm gonna go easy on you. You are hereby sentenced to five years of hard labor at Washington Correctional Institute. The sentence is to be run concurrent with your present seven-year sentence. Don't let me down."

He said that he didn't know why he was going easy on me. He didn't know, but I did. It was God. Jesus had come through! I've never been more excited in my whole life. I had been given a second chance at life for the second time, once by God and once by man. Soon I would be free!

I was excited all of the way back to WCI. The guards were happy too. It was a nice ride back. I stayed at WCI for six more months.

During that six months, Jeannie backslid. It tore me up. I had to go home, somehow. I prayed, asking God to make a way for me to go home, and He did. The warden scheduled me to go before the parole board. The board reviewed my records: I had been a model prisoner. I had only been written up one time. It was a minor violation, oversleeping. I explained to the board, "I was up late studying the Bible. I just overslept." They understood: God had blessed me again. I had paid my debt to society. They let me go home.

Life Today

Call upon Me in the day of trouble; I will deliveryou, and you shall glorify Me. (Psalm 50:15 NKJ)

Freedom is truly a precious gem, a God-given privilege of tremendous value. Many have paid dearly for freedom, yet it's so commonly taken for granted. As the time of my release approached, my mind was filled with optimism for the opportunity facing me. God had kept his end of the bargain. Soon, I would be free.

I spent the last couple of months in prison preparing to leave. I had accumulated a large quantity of Christian books. During family visitation, I began sending those books home. I began telling my friends good-bye. I prayed, and I made big plans. I had a vision for the future and would succeed.

My prison term officially ended at 12:00 p.m. on December 13, 1990. I carried my remaining possessions down the prison walk toward freedom. I passed through two electronic gates and stopped at the guard house. The guard returned my possessions, a ten dollar bill they had confiscated four years earlier. The clock ticked down to the famous 12:01, the convict's most anticipated moment, freedom. The gate swung open, the guard wished me well, and I walked out 12:01 a.m., December 14, 1990.

My wife stood waiting at the gate. I could hardly believe what was happening. I was free to go: free to hug her, to kiss her, to get in the car with her, and to go home! It was one of the greatest experiences of my life. It was answered prayer. I was free to go.

We stared at each other for a moment. It had been four years. We were practically strangers. Finally, I ran up to her, hugged her, kissed her, got in the car with her, and we left. Jeannie drove; I had no driver's license. We went home.

Jeannie was still in a backslidden state, so I started ministering to her right away. Almost immediately she repented and began living for God. Within a couple of months, she gave up cigarettes, the last vice. Since then, she's been continously growing in the grace and love of God. She's been a wonderful wife.

Life changed plenty while I was in prison. After several days of freedom, my family and I drove up to see my grandmother. We stopped to get gas, but I hadn't pumped gas in four years. It's amazing how fast things change. The pumps changed with the technology of the times. I didn't even know how to pump gas. Everything had changed.

I went through a big adjustment period. I found myself thrust into a society that had changed. I was accustomed to having guards tell me every move to make, and now I had to do things on my own. My wife went through a big adjustment period too. She had been making all of the decisions around the house, and now her role was changing. Our son had to adjust. His dad had always been in prison. It was a time of big change for us all.

Every step that I've taken, from then until now, has been ordered by the Lord. The Bible *says, "In all your ways acknowledge Him, and He shall direct your paths."* (Proverbs 3:6 NKJ). God has been with me every step of the way. At first, I was overwhelmed with responsibility. There was plenty that needed to be done. I went downtown and got a driver's license; driving was awkward at first. I searched through the want ads in the newspaper, and within three days I had a job doing paint and body repair.

The body and fender shop was located on North Street, a rough neighborhood in the inner city of Baton Rouge. Jeannie also had a job in Baton Rouge. Having only one car, she would drop me off an hour early each morning on her way to work. I would stand out front and wait for the shop to open. At night, she would have to wait for me to get off work. It was tough with one car, but we managed.

I worked long hours in a rough environment: cussing, fussing, complaining. The boss was not a Christian, and he didn't like me. It was tough. I was working myself to the bone, yet he steadily harassed me. I took it, I had to. We needed the money, the $240 per week.

During my first month out, I went down to the Sheriff's office and apologized to the Sheriff. It was a tough moment for us both; I had put them through so much. I made it quick. I just, simply told him that I was sorry for all that I had done. I assured him that he'd never have any further trouble from me. It was simply an "ice breaker" meeting.

After a couple of months of work, God gave me a vision, the only supernatural vision I've ever had. It was Friday, and I had just been paid. We were having trouble meeting our financial obligations. I began to pray about our situation and God told me to count my pay. I knew that it was only $240; my boss would never make a mistake with money, but in obedience to God, I counted it. I could hardly believe my eyes. It was $260. I counted it again, this time, $280. I knew that I hadn't miscounted; something supernatural was taking place. The money was multiplying in my hand. I yelled out to Jeannie, "Hey, come look!" I counted it again. There was only $240. God encouraged me, "This was simply a vision to show you my plan. From this day forward, I'm going to bless all that you do. You will prosper in everything." Several weeks later, I got a new job. The atmosphere was much nicer, and the pay, $275 per week.

We lived with Jeannie's aunt during my first couple of weeks of freedom. We slept on her couch. Finally, we were able to rent a trailer, a place of our own. We signed a six month lease and moved in. At the end of those six months, we bought a used double-wide trailer and nine acres of land. We moved in on the very day that the six month lease ran out. Our friends were shocked that we had gotten the loan. They couldn't believe it. God had really blessed us.

George and my mother were still living in my childhood home in Wakefield, Louisiana. My brother Chris was living there too. The drinking was really destroying their lives. I tried to tell my mother that, but she wouldn't listen. She already had cirrhosis of the liver once. The doctors had told her that she might live if she would quit drinking. She did quit for a short time, but eventually started back.

One day God spoke to me; he told me to go see my mother. I found her in the bed. She had been there for three days. It was cold in that house; she had nearly frozen to death. I wrapped her up in a blanket and took her to the hospital. They kept her for about a month. After being released, she stayed with us for about a month. She didn't drink during that month; she was really trying. She moved back in with George though, and before long, she was in bad shape again. Chris called for an ambulance one day, and they took her back to the hospital. She died the next day at the age of 47.

George continued to live in the house with Chris. I told him that he could stay if he would work. I tried to help him, but he wouldn't work. He wouldn't even clean up. He wouldn't do anything, except drink. I finally asked him to leave.

During our childhood, Chris was always esteemed as the favorable son, the one who would be successful. He made good grades and stayed out of trouble. He was calm, obedient, and respectful. It hurts me to see him plagued with the same spirit of addiction and revelry that oppressed me. It's a generational curse that has effected our whole family. I'm optimistic though; God is dealing with his heart, and I'm excited about the changes that are coming in his life.

I bought the house in Wakefield from Chris after my mother died, and we moved back in to straighten the place up. We had also inherited a trailer park there. Since then, we've remodeled the house and have turned the trailer park into a successful business.

My brother-in-law called me up in September of 1991 and began recruiting me for a job with his company. He was a successful salesman who was making good money. He told me that they had an opening, and that I should apply for a job. I did. Soon, they called me for an interview. It went great. They hired me on October 15, 1991. We were at the hospital when they called; Jeannie was giving birth to our second son, Zachary. It was a great day. God had blessed us with both a new son and a new job.

I soon began my new employment with this small, Louisiana-based company. The first year, I became their number one salesman. We've been extremely blessed ever since. The money has been great. I've had increases of 35% per year, every year. It's just phenomenal. God keeps our accountant busy. I remember filing taxes that first year. It was the first time I had ever filed. I told the accountant I had been a drug smuggler all of my life and had just gotten out of prison. She couldn't believe it. She didn't know what to do. The IRS didn't even know that I existed.

I remained the number one salesman with my company until the acquisition. We were bought out by a large corporation, a nationwide company. That year, I was ranked number 10 in sales for the entire nation. The following year, I was number four out of 1,500 sales people. God is so good!

I've learned that the key to getting is giving. That's the message of Luke 6:38. It's the way to get the blessings of God. I've learned, to be more specific, that it's not only giving, but giving to people, being a servant to people. That's what really moves God's heart. If you serve people, God will most definitely bless you. It works every time.

We've had the privilege of giving several cars to needy people over the last few years; we also buy groceries to help people in need. We always give in the name of Jesus, and it keeps coming back to us. We tithe 10% before taxes, and then give offerings above the tithe. We give and God gives back. It's incredible. Money just seems to come from everywhere. It's the law of reaping and sowing, and it works. You can't out give God!

During my first week out of prison, I got involved with a local church. I worshipped there about a year. During the end of that year, God began speaking to my heart about changing churches. He was calling me to be a servant of people. So one Sunday morning, I took my family to another local church. After the service, I told Jeannie that this would be our church. She agreed. We were there for about 7 years

I am totally sold out to Jesus. I spend my life serving both God and man. I've taken many people into my home over these years. We've moved entire families into our home for months at a time. We took in an 18 year-old one time. We took in a 14 year-old another. We just try to help people. I believe that the mission of a Christian is to win souls. I live that way. That's my purpose for being here on planet Earth. It's not about money, fame, or fortune. It's not about promoting to the next job. It's about souls, winning souls to Jesus.

I've used my trailer park, to some extent, as a ministry. I own five of the trailers there. We've tried to be selective with the people that rent them. I like renting them to people in need, people that will go to church with us. It's so good to see people come to Jesus, to see them set free.

One time we took in Wally, his wife, and two children. They were homeless when we met them. We moved them into our home for about three months. I helped him get a job in Baton Rouge, then rented them one of our trailers. Jeannie drove him back and forth to work. They were doing good, until they decided to go back into the world. They didn't stick with Jesus and things started down hill for them. They started drinking and drugging again and consequently are no longer together. The last time I saw Wally, he had just gotten out of jail for taking someone else's car across three state lines.

You've got to stay the course. Sin will always take you further than you planned to go, keep you longer than you planned to stay, and cost you more than you planned to pay.

I've been blessed with a terrific family. Zachary, my five year-old, walks around the house singing, "Shake the devil off." He's quite a character. Stirling, our 11 year-old, makes straight A's in school. I recently rented a stretch limousine to pick up him and a couple of his friends from school. He had a lot of fun. In my opinion, he deserved it; I never made an "A" in my entire life. Both of our kids are saved, thank God. I'm raising them a little bit differently from the way I was raised.

Jeannie is the most wonderful woman in the world. Her life is a ministry. She does a lot of intercessory prayer behind the scenes. She's washed dishes and clothes for people staying in our home and has never complained, not once. We've both been hurt badly by people that have stayed here, people that we've gotten close to, that have gone back out into the world. It hurts, but Jeannie has never complained. We just keep on doing it.

I could spend another 500 pages talking about my wife. She loves people. That's the bottom line. She's constantly cooking for people, praying with people, praying for people, taking people places, ministering to people, counseling people. She visits people in the hospital. She doesn't even think that she's doing anything special. She thinks that every Christian is doing what she does, but it's just not so. If every Christian did what my wife does, this world would not be in the shape that it's in. She's a precious wife. She's a wonderful woman. She takes care of every need that my kids and I have. We love her much.

We serve people, that's what we do. Our motto is "Win the lost at any cost, because people last forever." It costs us our time, our money, our

privacy, and everything else, but it's worth it. That's
what we do. We serve people. It doesn't matter
what race, weight, height, name, religion,
reputation, or anything else; we serve people. Jesus
said, "Let the greatest among you be servants."
That's what it's all about, serving people.

I've been living for Jesus for nearly 10 years
now. During prison my nickname was Jimmy
Swaggart. They called me "little Jimmy." They'd
say, "There goes little Jimmy. He's hiding behind
that Bible. When he gets out, he'll never pick that
Bible up again." But they were wrong. I went back
to preach at WCI several years after my parole. I
reminded them, "Everybody said I'd leave this
Bible at the gate when I got out, but I've got news
for you: not only did I take it home with me, I
also brought it back tonight." I've served Jesus
as long as I served the devil, and man is it a better
life. There's no comparison.

People ask me sometimes, "Ricky, do you
think you'll ever go back?" And I'll answer, "Go
back???!!!! Go back to what? Go back to hugging
a commode? Go back to overdosing? Back to
prison? Are you crazy? Of course not! I'm
sticking with Jesus."

I always try to witness to everyone that I see.
It's the most important thing that you can ever do

for anybody. I know that Jesus is truly the only answer; He's changed my life. So, I just strike up a conversation like this, "Praise the Lord! Praise the Lord! What about Jesus?" I'm a nut for Jesus! Why not? Why not go all out for Him? He died for you and me.

I have problems in life like everybody else, but I try to keep a good attitude. Our attitude is the most important thing that we have. I always try to encourage myself to smile and to be upbeat. Depression is of the devil, and I'm at war with him.

The Bible says, *"Let love be without hypocrisy. Abhor what is evil. Cling to what is good."* (**Romans 12:9** NKJ) That's how I live, always. It doesn't matter who I'm around; I abhor every form of evil. I just don't have anything at all to do with the devil. I'm a Christian; I live for Jesus everywhere, around anybody. I'm not a lizard Christian. I hope to preach a sermon on lizards one day. I don't change colors. I just love Jesus, and I love you.

Closing Comments

At this point, you've probably just read this true life account of the Ricky Sinclair story. I've witten this story in the first person, from Ricky's viewpoint. My only source of information thus far has been Ricky and Jeannie. The majority of the story occurred many years ago. With this in mind, I decided that it would be good to interview some people that knew Ricky both then and now. I wanted to see how they recalled it. I talked with Sheriff Bill Daniel, Officer Ernest James, Chase Team Captain Bobby Olibeaux, and judge Wilson Ramshur. They each gave me their version. I also interviewed Brother Jonathon Samuel, a former pastor of Ricky's.

Sheriff Daniel, West Feliciana Parish, Louisiana

If there was ever a survivor, it would have to be Ricky Sinclair. He's truly a survivor. I'm sure that he could teach the United States Army a trick or two about survival.

He ran out of our jail on April 21, 1987. We had just brought him here on charges of distribution of marijuana. He had bonded out of jail in St. Bernard Parish. We picked him up there, delivered him to our court, and then took him to the jail. After using the telephone, he ran out the front door. Our deputies chased him, but he got away. We immediately called the Angola search team. We also called in some helicopters. Everybody we could get was involved with the search. He was on the run from April 21 to June 15, 1987. He survived in the woods for nearly two months.

On June 15, we got a lead from someone that had seen Ricky. We caught him at his mother's home in Wakefield. He was in the attic. One of my deputies went into the attic and got him. He told me that he had survived off of raw animals: armadillos, frogs, that kind of stuff. He ate raw turnips and dewberries. He even made some dewberry wine. He had really lost a lot of weight.

Ricky had been involved with drugs for a number of years. He had previously been in our jail on drug distribution charges. He's really had a hard life, but I believe that he's finally got it together today. From what I can tell, he's living a clean life. He's on the right track. He's active in his church. He studies the Bible. I just hope he'll stick with it.

He found a pistol in his yard one day while mowing his grass. Obviously, someone had thrown it in Ricky's yard. He called our office and asked us to come get it. We did.

On a separate occasion, an escaped convict went to Ricky's house to seek advice. Ricky convinced the guy to turn himself in and then called our office. We went out there and picked him up. Ricky is really doing good. I understand that he's the number one salesman in Louisiana with his company. I'm happy for him. I hope that he'll continue to do good. Ricky Sinclair has definitely changed.

Officer Ernest James, West Feliciana Parish, Louisiana

I had heard of Ricky Sinclair, but I had never met him. The first time I recall seeing Ricky, well up close, was when they brought him here to jail. I was over at the computer. I was running a driver's license check. Ricky was either on the phone or in the bathroom. I can't remember which. I do remember him hitting that front door though. Man, he was really moving. We chased him, but he got away. We called for a search team, bloodhounds and helicopters.

When we caught him, he had lost a lot of weight. He was really thin, and man did he have an appetite. You didn't have to force him to eat. By the time he left here, going to prison, he had put most of his weight back on. He might have even been a little bit on the heavy side.

If I had to describe Ricky Sinclair in one word, I would use the word "tough." That's Ricky in a nutshell. He was a great high school athlete. I do remember that. He could have gone somewhere in football. He was little, but man was he tough. He's one guy that I'd hate to ever have to fight. I believe there are very few people that would have wanted to fight him, one on one, that day he escaped. He was ripping out of here like a madman.

When he was in jail here, after the escape, I gave him a Bible that his mother brought down here. He started reading it. He was searching for answers. Being a born again Christian, I began to witness to him about Jesus. I love all people, black or white, whoever. I love both the good and the bad. That's why I witnessed to him, and fortunately was able to lead him to the Lord.

Ricky was saved that day. I mean really saved. I brought Bible studies to him. He'd take the test.

Our pastor graded them. Ricky scored as high as anybody in our church, higher than most.

Ricky is one of my best friends today. God has really changed him. About nine years after receiving Christ, Ricky came and preached at my church. It was a powerful message. He's a good preacher. He's a good guy. You can believe that everything that Ricky has told you in this book is exactly like he recalls it. He's honest. I can't wait to read this book.

Mr. Bobby Oliveaux, Chase Team Captain, Louisiana State Penitentiary, Angola, Louisiana

I've known Ricky all of his life. His dad owned a meat packing company. My dad was good friends with his dad. I had heard that Ricky was into drugs, but I really didn't know the extent of it. The whole thing kind of caught me by surprise. The sheriff's office called me to come chase him down. He had escaped from jail. I chased him all around this parish. You could hear him up ahead of the dogs. He was running through briars and brush. He sounded like a bull running through that stuff. I know the briars and branches must have really torn up his arms and face.

Ricky stayed in the woods for many weeks eating raw armadillos, frogs, and no telling what else. We weren't chasing him the whole time. We all had other things to do. I had to go to my regular job at Angola. Occasionally, someone would call in with an alleged sighting, and we would go out and chase him again. Chasing Ricky was like chasing a rabbit in his own briar patch. He knew where he was, and where he was going.

Since prison, Ricky Sinclair has really been a changed man. I worked at Angola for 27 years. I've been around convicts all my life. I grew up around 'em. I've seen convicts try to use the Bible to get favor with the parole board. It happens all the time. You can tell which ones are sincere and which ones aren't. Ricky Sinclair is sincere. I've seen him on several different occasions since his prison term. He's got that glow in his eyes. You can tell that what he has is real. In addition to that, he doesn't have any harbored hatred or resentment. He just seems to know that chasing him was my job, and he doesn't have a problem with it, though most of 'em do.

The first time I saw him after prison, he acted like he was glad to see me. I know that he's really a Christian. If I needed help with something, I could call Ricky Sinclair right now and he'd be here. I'm sure of that. He's a friend. He's also a pleasure to be around. He's a nice, happy-go-lucky, smiling type guy. You couldn't ask for anyone nicer to be around. He's really changed.

Judge Wilson Ramshur, West Feliciana Parish, Louisiana

Ricky has always been a personable type of guy. The whole time that I've been on this bench, he's treated me with courtesy and respect. That's the way that Ricky has always been. The way that he deals with people really hasn't changed. Ricky has always been a friendly guy.

As far as I know, he was never a violent person. The drugs were the thing with Ricky. He just insisted on dealing drugs. Apparently, he didn't think that there was anything wrong with that. He spent some time in jail with no demonstrable signs of improvement. Of course you know about the escape. He lived in the woods for several months. The sheriff's office caught him in the attic of his mother's house.

His dad died while he was in jail on drug charges. At his mother's request, we released him early to attend the funeral. Almost immediately he was back in the drugs. It took a prison experience to bring him to the point of examining his life and deciding that he wanted to change. At some point during prison, he had Christ revealed to him. He made a decision to accept Christ, and subsequently, has made some very significant changes in his lifestyle. This is one instance in which the process, at least with the help of the good Lord, has worked.

Mr. Jonathon Samuel, Assistant Pastor, District I, Bethany World Prayer Center, Baker, Louisiana

Ricky Sinclair is a genuine man of God. When I first met Ricky, five years ago, I didn't know what to think. He was completely different from anyone that I'd ever met. He had a zeal about him. I didn't know if it was just an act or the real thing. Over the years, I've found out that it's definitely the real thing. Jesus said that we are to be disciplers of men. Ricky is a discipler. He'll move entire families into his home to minister Jesus to them. I know of at least 4 families that he's taken in. He's taken in drug addicts, alcoholics, and homeless people right off the streets. He gives and gives and gives of himself, and that's the character of God in him. He lays down his life for people, and that's what God wants us to do.

Ricky has taken in people that, quite frankly, I wouldn't have moved into my house. I've had to counsel Ricky about this on several occasions. I told him that he needed to take time for himself and his family. I told him that he couldn't help everyone, that he has an obligation to himself and his family. Since then, he's gotten a better balance between discipling and family. I've seen his zeal mellow out with wisdom, but he still takes people in.

I love Ricky; I think a whole lot of him. He's always asking, "Brother, what can I do for you? Do you need anything? I love you, brother! If I can do anything for you, let me know, brother." He's always thinking about the other person: "Can I serve you? Do you need anything? How can I help you?"

I really appreciate Ricky. I'd like to have an army of Ricky Sinclairs. We would win this world quick if we had an army full of people like Ricky. He's really a person to be admired. And he has so much energy. I told him one time, "Ricky, if we could plug a 440 line into you somehow, there'd be enough electricity to supply all of Baton Rouge." He loves people. He takes the bull by the horns. I've tried to help him learn to pace himself. He just goes and goes and goes. He's the same type person as the Apostle Paul. He's not going to wait around on someone else. He's gonna go ahead and do it himself. I'm afraid that he's going to burn himself out, but so far he hasn't. God is using him in a mighty way. Ricky is a man after God's heart. I would recommend Ricky to any ministry, any pastor, or any church. If everyone strived to do the will of God like Ricky does, it would be a great world.

The Ricky Sinclair story is truly an amazing demonstration of the grace and love of the Lord Jesus Christ. Though circumstances may differ, we each have things in our past that have separated us from God. In the New Testament, the Bible says:

"For all have sinned and fall short of the glory of God." (Romans 3:23 NKJ) It also says:

"There is none righteous, no, not one;" (Romans 3:10 NKJ); and: *"For the wages of sin is death, but the gift of God is eternal life in Christ Jesus our Lord."* (Romans 6:23 NKJ)

As a sinful person with a sin debt, the only hope that we have for being reconciled to God is through the blood of Jesus Christ. You see, the good news is that Jesus Christ has come, has died to reconcile us to God, and has risen from the dead. He's alive today and is seated at the right hand of God. His righteousness is available to cover your sin. He shed his blood for that. It's available to any and all that ask for it. He wants to save you. That was his purpose for coming to planet Earth, to save you. If you would like to receive Jesus as Savior and Lord, simply pray the following sinner's prayer in a sincere manner. Pray out loud.

Father God:

I know that I've sinned against you, that I've fallen short of your glory and honor. I know that there are things in my life that need to be changed. I've never had success in changing these things on my own.

I know that the Bible is the true Word of God. In it, you promise salvation to whosoever will believe in Jesus and ask him to save them.

Therefore Father, I have decided to ask Jesus to be the Lord of my life. In the name of Jesus, I am asking you to please forgive my past. Help me change the areas that are not pleasing to you and give me a desire to do the right thing. I confess that Jesus Christ is Lord. Thank you Father.

In Jesus' Name I Pray. Amen.

If you're not presently attending a good, Bible-teaching church, I would like to close by encouraging you to do so. If you are in the Greater Baton Rouge Area, I welcome you to visit with us at our church:

Miracle Place Church
2080 Highway 19
Baker, Louisiana 70714

(on the corner of Baker Boulevard and
 Highway 19)
(225) 775-4321

We are non-denominational and offer contemporary praise, exciting children's church, a safe nursery and state of the art youth facilities. You will see people from all walks of life-from suits to bluejeans-come just the way you are.

If you would like me to come do motivational speaking or to come share my testimony with your organization or church, or if you would like to obtain a copy of this book, please call or write. We recommend a suggested donation of $5 per book to help defray the cost of printing and shipping. For your convenience, you may order with your VISA or MasterCard. Please use the form in the back of this book or contact us at the number and address above.

I speak the blessing of God over every area of your life-

-Ricky Sinclair

Share with us-

If you have decided to be born again and make Jesus the Lord of your life as the result of reading this book, we would like to know about it. Please fill out this coupon and return it to us so we may share in your joy.

Name: _____

Address: _____

Comments: _____

_____

_____

_____

_____

_____

Sinclair World Ministries
P.O. Box 19
Wakefield, LA 70784
swmonline.org

Help Index

Facing a Crisis
    Psalm 121
    Matt. 6:25-34
    Heb. 4:16
Faith Falls
    Psalm 42:5
    Heb. 11
Falsehood
    Rev. 21:8
    II Pet. 2:19
Faultfinding
    Matt. 7:1-5
Flesh
    Rom. 13:14
    Rom. 8:5-9
Friends fail
    Psalm 41:9-13
    Luke 17:3-4
    Rom. 12:14,17,19,21
    II Tim. 4:16-18
Hatred
    Matt. 5:11-12
Lonely
    Psalm 23
    Heb. 13:5-6
Lust
    Mark 4:18,19
    Eph. 4:20-24
    Gal. 5:19-21

Needing God's Protection
    Psalm 27:1-6
    Psalm 91
    Phil. 4:19
Needing Guidance
    Psalm 32:8
    Prov. 3:5-6
    John 14:26
Needing Peace
    John 14:1-4
    John 16:33
    Rom. 5:1-5
    Phil. 4:6-7
Needing Rules for Living
    Romans 12
    II Peter 1:3-10
Overcome
    Rom. 8:31-39
    Rev. 12:11
Persecution
    Matt. 5:43-48
Prayer
    Psalm 4
    Luke 11:1-13
    John 17
    I John 5:14-15
Pride
    I John 2:15-17
    I Tim. 3:6
    James 4:16

Protected
Psalm 18:1-3
Psalm 34:7
Revenge
Matt. 5:43-38
Heb. 10:30
Rom. 12:17-21
Sick or in Pain
Psalm 38
James 5:14-15
Rom. 8:28,38-39
II Cor. 12:9-10
I Peter 4:12,13,19
Sorrowful
Psalm 51
Matt. 5:4
II Cor. 1:3-4
Spiritual War
Eph. 6:11-18
II Cor. 10:3-5
Temptation
I Cor. 10:13
James 1:12-16
Tempted
Matt. 26:41
I Cor. 10:12-14
Phil. 4:8
James 4:7-8
11 Peter 2:9
II Peter 3:17

Thankful
Psalm 100
I Thes. 5:18
Thoughts
Phil. 4:8
Traveling
Psalm 121
Trials
I Peter 1:7
I Peter 4:12
Tribulation
John 16:33
II Cor. 1:3-4
Trouble, in
Psalm 16
John 14:1-4
Heb. 7:25
Weary
Psalm 90
Matt. 11:28-30
I Cor. 15:58
Gal. 6:9-10
Worldliness
I John 2:15-17
I Tim. 6:6-12
Worried
Matt. 6:19-34
I Peter 5:6-7

Become a Faithful Team Member of Sinclair World Ministries!!!

For your monthly commitment of $20 or more we'll send you a SWM t-shirt absolutely free.

Dear Sinclair World Ministries,
I would like to be a monthly supporter and sow a seed of faith for:

_____ $25 _____ $10 _____ $100 _____ other

I would like to give a one time gift of $ _____
I am in prayer for you _____
**Please write your prayer request on back of form!!

_____
Name

_____
Address

_____
City   State   Zip

_____
Phone Number

_____
Email Address

Credit Card:
___ ___ VISA _____ Mastercard Expiration Date: _____

Card No.: _____

Signature: _____

**Sinclair World Ministries is a Nonprofit Organization
Your gift is tax deductible!**

Sinclair World Ministries
P.O. Box 19 • Wakefield, LA 70784
(225) 635-6426 • Webpage: swmonline.org